# JUST KIDDING!

# JOKES AND More

## About Horses

By Maria Nelson

Gareth Stevens
PUBLISHING

Please visit our website, www.garethstevens.com. For a free color catalog of all our high-quality books, call toll free 1-800-542-2595 or fax 1-877-542-2596.

**Library of Congress Cataloging-in-Publication Data**

Nelson, Maria.
Jokes and more about horses / by Maria Nelson.
   p. cm. — (Just kidding!)
Includes index.
ISBN 978-1-4824-0549-1 (pbk.)
ISBN 978-1-4824-3324-1 (6-pack)
ISBN 978-1-4824-0548-4 (library binding)
1. Wit and humor, Juvenile. 2. Horses — Miscellanea — Juvenile literature. I. Nelson, Maria. II. Title.
PN6163.N45 2014
818—dc23

First Edition

Published in 2015 by
**Gareth Stevens Publishing**
111 East 14th Street, Suite 349
New York, NY 10003

Designer: Sarah Liddell
Editor: Kristen Rajczak

Photo credits: Cover, p. 1 Studio 37/Shutterstock.com; pp. 5, 12 Nate Allred/Shutterstock.com; pp. 6 (top horse), 9 (right horse), 13 (right horse), 14 (left horse), 17 (right horse), 18 (right horse) insima/Shutterstock.com; p. 6 (bottom horse) HitToon.com/Shutterstock.com; pp. 7, 19 Sari ONeal/Shutterstock.com; p. 8 Horse Crazy/Shutterstock.com; p. 9 (left horse) iaRada/Shutterstock.com; p. 10 (right horse) Sarawut Padungkwan/Shutterstock.com; pp. 10 (left horse), 13 (left horse), 14 (right horse), 17 (left horse), 18 (left horse) Igor Zakowski/Shutterstock.com; p. 11 PaulyShlykov/Shutterstock.com; p. 15 Elena Sherengovskaya/Shutterstock.com; p. 16 Alexandra Lande/Shutterstock.com; p. 20 LacoKozyna/Shutterstock.com; p. 21 Alexia Khruscheva/Shutterstock.com; p. 22 (top horse) kosam/Shutterstock.com; p. 22 (bottom horse) Anastasija Popova/Sutterstock.com.

Printed in the United States of America

CPSIA compliance information: Batch #CS15GS: For further information contact Gareth Stevens, New York, New York at 1-800-542-2595.

# Contents

Words in the glossary appear in **bold** type the first time they are used in the text.

# Horsing Around

There is only one species, or kind, of horse, but there are about 400 different **breeds**. From the huge Clydesdale to the tiny Shetland pony, all these breeds have different features and **temperaments**. Horses are known for having very clear personalities. That means if they don't want to jump a fence, their rider might be flying over it without them!

People and horses have been working well together for thousands of years. That doesn't stop the horses—or people—from acting silly sometimes!

# The Need for Speed

What do you feed a racehorse?
Fast food.

A racehorse was waiting at the starting gate of the Kentucky Derby.

It said to its rider, "It's hot! I hope we won't be out here **furlong**!"

What is the best story to tell a runaway horse?
A tale of WHOA!

# All Kinds

What kinds of horses only come out after sunset?

Nightmares.

8

What's a horse's favorite type of bread?
Thoroughbred.

A girl's mother said she couldn't have a horse.

The girl said, "Not even a quarter horse? There's less to take care of!"

What kind of horse enjoys a windy day?
A **draft** horse.

# Feeling Lucky?

Is it safe to stand behind a horse?

Give it a try. You'll get a kick out of it!

Do horses wear pajamas?
No, but they do wear shoes to bed.

What does it mean if you find a horseshoe in the road?
Some poor horse is walking around in socks!

10

# Horsey Terms

Which part of the horse is most important?

The mane part.

What do you do when a horse is getting married?
Have a **bridle** shower.

Who rode a horse up a hill to fetch a pail of water?

Jockey and Jill.

What animal has more **hands** than feet?
A horse!

# Name of the Game

What's the fastest way to ship a horse?
Pony Express.

A man rode to town on Friday. The next day, he rode home on Friday. How is this possible?

His horse's name is Friday.

What kind of horse comes from Pennsylvania?
A Philly.

What's a horse's favorite football team?

The Colts.

15

# Just Sayin'

What did the horse say when it finished its breakfast?
"That's the last straw!"

How did the pony explain the broken stable door to its mother?

"I was just horsing around!"

What did the pony with the sore throat say?
"I'm a little hoarse."

One horse called to its friend that was sleeping in,
"Giddyup already, you're going to be late!"

17

# Down and Out

Why was the young horse sad?
Its mother always said "neigh!"

What illness is a horse scared of catching?

Hay fever.

What do you do with a blue horse?
Cheer him up!

# Final Funnies

How do horses like to wear their hair?
In ponytails.

What do you call the horse next door?
A neigh-bor!

# Fun and Funny Facts About Horses

Horses can't burp. They can't throw up, either. Their **digestive system** only goes in one way and out another!

A horse can see almost all the way behind and in front of itself because its eyes are on the sides of its head. That's not the only cool fact about horses' eyes: they have the biggest eyes of any land animal!

All ponies are horses, but not all horses are ponies! The difference between them is simply size. Ponies are less than 14.2 hands high. That's about 4 feet 9 inches (1.4 m) tall.

Have you ever heard of a zorse? It's the offspring of a horse and a zebra, which are in the same animal family. A zorse looks a lot like a horse with stripes!

# Glossary

**breed:** a group of animals that share features different from other groups of the same kind

**bridle:** a set of straps used for controlling a horse that fit around its head and mouth

**digestive system:** the parts of the body used to break down food

**draft:** used for pulling loads. Also, a current of air.

**furlong:** a unit of length equal to 660 feet (201 m) often used in horse racing

**hand:** the unit of measurement used for horses. One hand is equal to 4 inches (10.2 cm).

**jockey:** someone who rides a racehorse

**temperament:** nature

# For More Information

## BOOKS

Behling, Silke. *Get to Know Horse Breeds: The 100 Best-Known Breeds.* Berkeley Heights, NJ: Enslow Publishers, 2014.

Burns, Diane L., et al. *Horsing Around: Jokes to Make Ewe Smile.* Minneapolis, MN: Carolrhoda Books, 2005.

## WEBSITES

**All Horse Breeds**
*www.horsechannel.com/horse-breeds/all_landing.aspx*
Read all about the many kinds of horses.

**Discoverhorses.com: Games & Quizzes**
*www.discoverhorses.com/kids/games-quizzes/*
Play games and do puzzles while learning all about horses and horseback riding.